# HOTCHPOTCH

# HOTCH POTCH

SONNETS, IDYLLS
& RANDOM BEMUSEMENTS

Christopher Askew

**MERANO WRITERS PRESS**
LOS ANGELES

Copyright © 2019 by Christopher Askew

All rights reserved. No part of this book may be reproduced or transmitted in any form or by any means, electronic or mechanical, including photocopying, scanning, recording, or by an information storage and retrieval system - except by a reviewer who may quote brief passages in a review to be printed in a magazine or newspaper - without permission in writing from the author. Your support of the author's rights is appreciated. Any member of an educational institution wishing to reproduce part or all of the work for classroom use, or anthology, should send inquiries to permissions@meranowriterspress.com.

Cover art by Marielle Askew

Book design by Christopher Askew

ISBN 978-1-949713-11-4

Merano Writers Press
Los Angeles, CA
www.meranowriterspress.com

## Acknowledgements

This book would not exist without the unfaltering encouragement of the Merano Writers Group in Pasadena and is dedicated to everyone who has poked and prodded and shamed me into creating it. Special thanks to my daughter Marielle for getting me to go in the first place, to Dr. Bernie De Paolis for keeping me from giving up, and to her students for keeping me honest.

Grateful acknowledgement is also made to the following publications in which these previously uncollected poems first appeared:

*Altadena Poetry Review Anthology 2019:* Barista; Canyon Crows; Why Talk That Way

*Spectrum*: Michele'd Better Call Me; Blow Out; In Wildness; Scarecrow

# Contents

## ONE

There Is A Place .................................................................. 3
Canyon Crows ..................................................................... 4
Joseph ................................................................................. 6
Paradise Retained ............................................................... 8
Goodbye And ...................................................................... 9
Nona Nods ........................................................................ 10
Morning Tale .................................................................... 12
Pulling Weeds on an Autumn Afternoon ........................ 13
Brahman ........................................................................... 14
Sierra ................................................................................ 15

## TWO

Afternoon Nap ................................................................. 19
Cartouche (The Seal) ....................................................... 20
Evening Comes ................................................................ 21
Morning After .................................................................. 22
Rear-view ......................................................................... 23
Michele'd Better Call Me ................................................ 24
Masakr u Srebrenici ........................................................ 25
Garden Meditation on Atomic Theory ........................... 26
Intentions ......................................................................... 27
Littered ............................................................................ 28
In Wildness ...................................................................... 29
Short-staffed .................................................................... 30

Stone .................................................................... 31

Legacy .................................................................. 32

Vexed ................................................................... 33

## THREE

Under Construction ............................................... 37

Agnosia ................................................................ 38

Terrible Twos ........................................................ 39

If Only ................................................................. 40

Tin Man ............................................................... 41

Scarecrow ............................................................ 42

Pet the Cat ........................................................... 43

You Had Me at Goodbye ...................................... 46

2 Close 2 Home .................................................... 47

The Kindness ....................................................... 48

Lent ..................................................................... 49

Medi-cares ........................................................... 50

Poesis .................................................................. 51

The Tangerine Tree .............................................. 52

Small Duties ........................................................ 53

Don't Speak ......................................................... 54

Given ................................................................... 55

## FOUR

For A Time .......................................................... 59

Barista ................................................................. 60

Jonah ................................................................... 61

My Kingdom ........................................................ 62

Governing In The New Millennium ....................... 63
Coasting ..................................................... 64
'Twas A Wonderful Life ........................................... 65
Blow Out .................................................... 66
Why Talk That Way? ............................................... 67
Fluff ........................................................ 68
Stopping On The Verge Of An Intimate Evening 69
Market Ethics .............................................. 70
War & Peace ................................................ 71
Index of Poems ........................................ 75

# ONE

# There Is A Place

there is a place
where sun and wind collide
with towering fortresses of rock and cloud
and time and rivers flowing
carve in ruddy plains deep spaces
vast and clear

in one such deep a hollow curves
a dimple in the palm of God

outside
the pageant of Creation plays
in billowing robes of rust and gold
on piercing fiercest blue
the fanfare of the bright and boisterous air

inside there's calm:
a flower grows

one day I'll take you there
and, backs against the sheltering stone
faces to the flow
we'll listen 'til words wear away
and rest on silence,
safe and whole.

## Canyon Crows

Before the first dogs bark
   the rim's birds
      break the still fast
         of the chill canyon dawn

   finch junco sparrow towhee
   stir hop chirrup rustle trill
      fresh daily domesticity
         in cholla piñon juniper

  Across the canyon's vast
    and warming silence
       down the gilding gorge
         a solitary crow
      on purpled stillness glides

     away up-canyon
        slides another
   silvered feathers flash
      the splash of river far below
         calling stretching reaching

They meet to wheel to twine
   as one on up-shot air
      whirling soaring wing to wing
         in close formation for a time

   then spiraling weaving
     climbing falling
        chasing sun-tide
         down deep craggy walls
     twist turn rise again
        to shoot the rimless heights
       and chant the music
         of the morning

      Too soon
    the glorious birds
depart, first one
    and then the other vanishing
        in ever-brightening
            newly-risen Light

      leaving rim birds
          and the (now less) silent dogs
        seared memories
          of fearless flight
        and echoes of brash songs.

*In memory of Harold and Jean*

## Joseph

Golden oak
soft-scented cedar
companions of my day
sharp iron, keen eye
my tools, strong arms
gnarled hands
sun-warped rough rail
the heft and touch
of beam, block, board
post, hook, nail -
with such the framework
for a solitary life I lay

Then
through that frame of habit,
age-strained wall
made hard and fast by passing years
there came
crashing
first an angel
then this tiny child
who with one smile
my wild and anxious
thoughts could tame
and build in me new purpose
once for all.

O spirit-child
O God rough-hewn
entrusted to my care this starry night
to shape and smooth
and send upon your way
like father, son –

a carpenter you'll be one day
though hearts not hearths you heal
not walls but worlds
your plumb-line set aright.

# Paradise Retained

*Inspired by a New Yorker cartoon*

While she knew God's forbearance was great, without measure
One bite of that apple would make her a sinner
So rather than risk the Creator's displeasure
Eve skewered the snake and they had it for dinner.

# Goodbye And...

*An acrostic*

Goodbye, good friend, it's time for you to go
Of making merry we have had our share
Our tales we told, our cups did overflow
Diverting us while autumn's hours fell bare.

Remember on that far fair summer's day
I met you on the road and bid you bide?
Did I know then how generous your stay
Despite my errands I'd have stayed inside.

And now drear winter's weeks grow wan and chill
Now too my patience and my cellar's store
Come short, and though I'll love each visit still
Each absence will endear you even more.

# Nona Nods

*Nona - the spinner of the thread of life — with her sisters Decima and Morta are the three Fates of Roman and Greek mythology, the controllers of human destiny. They are sometimes associated with the Temple of Apollo and its oracle at Delphi, which sits on the slopes of Mount Parnassus above the seaside town of Itea.*

Beneath her careful fingers stiches fly—
*Delphic geese across a* rasa *sky—*
Nona nods, unfurls and smooths
fresh cloth and through the needle's eye
unspools a new-spun thread.

The Singer whirls and hums, the fabric flows:
a onesie's tiny ducks-all-in-a-row becomes
a prom dress' late judicious dart—
*a swelling heart requires accommodation—*

Nona nods; with gentle concentration
seams of jeans' patched knees—
torn climbing trees—trim the floating
veil on summer's bride—

a white-bleached curtain billowing wide
to let Itea's sun and sea breeze through—
*what's Seen is never certain, ever new—*

Nona nods, and smock and apron,
frock and gown, suit and shawl
unfold, each sewn with all
the toil and joy a life can hold.

Now sunset gilds Parnassus
Nona nods, and as she bends
she knots and snips the thread—
*a life well led*—selects another
pattern and begins again.

# Morning Tale

*What if Romeo and Juliet, or Hamlet and Ophelia, had made it past the infighting in-laws and the honeymoon and managed to settle down? How would it have worked, real life in iambic pentameter, each conversation rife with allusion and double-entendre? For example, a guy just wants to say "Not now, hon, I gotta go to work"...*

Sweet huntress, stay thy gentle, hindering hand
And leave me from Love's tender toils be loosed;
A clarion Duty summons me apart
From slyly snaring sheets. For lo!
How Eos' blushing balm anoints the skies
And Phoebus from his eastward couch doth rise
To fasten flaming steed to chariot of fire
And mount the meadows of the morn!

Seek not to bridle me with lustrous tress
While 'pon thy lap, my love, thy liege I lay;
A moment's dalliance, and I in Morpheus'
Bosom, like the grateful dead should lie,
Unmoving and unmoved. Nay, fardels must
I bear, to grunt and sweat 'neath wearier load
Than thee; my horn unpolishéd, I flee,
Or woe betide.

*Laisse, laisse! O laisse!*
If ever thou dost my great fortune love
Let slip my bonds and pray me on my way
While thou may'st bide and rest to later rise
To this, a brighter day!

# Pulling Weeds on an Autumn Afternoon

This garden was the place I'd go
when I had little else to do;
I used to love to wander through
its wildness when my day was slow.

Some days I'd find the gardener, who
would shake his head and smile at me
then, parting leaves, he'd help me see
a bursting bud afire with dew.

Now slow days come less frequently;
I seldom find the gardener here;
tall tangled weeds now interfere
where once the wonders used to be.

The leaves pile high this time of year
when hours and energy come dear
but when I stop and stoop and clear
the weeds away, the flowers show.

# Brahman

*A simple shape poem. Brahman is the Hindu ur-deity, the absolute, the divine ground of all being, in essence eternal, indivisible, immutable and transcendent. The equal-sided triangle suggests the Trimurti, the threefold personification of the eternal as Brahma the creator, Vishnu the sustainer, and Shiva the destroyer.*

```
                    I
                   am
                  one
                  that
                 is by
                art no
               man can
              sever my
              essential
             truth into
             constituent
            atomies I am
           the fundament
           of all that is
          In me there can
          be no separation
         no component part
        for of diversities
        I am the foundation
```

## Sierra

rise wild
bones of earth
thrust proud
cloud sweep
made fist
strike high
bright peak
on peak
sky kissed

ice breath
in rush
to seep
clear soft
down soul's
dark rift
reach deep
stone hush
and weary
spirits lift

# TWO

## Afternoon Nap

*Mais où sont les sommes d'antan – a (re)tired François Villon*

*Au temps jadis*, a nap seemed such a luxury.
Used to be *l'après-midi* raged *furioso* –
meeting after meeting, breaks a rarity, so
feet up? No way. Head down? Impossible.

On those scarce days when headlong minutes slowed
to luscious dappled hours – when blest s*iestes*
refreshed with lotus-petal showers a mind
obsessed, and languorous quiet flowed – who would
have guessed all afternoons could be *lentissimo*'d –
*sans* measure save an inching toward the grave?

*At leisure* shredded to a thousand dreaded
*nows*, a nap bestows no pleasure – rather
scant repose from ghosts of meetings past
and flight from fears that those will be the last.

# Cartouche
# (The Seal)

*The result [of academicization] is a poetry that is neither robust, resonant, nor—and I stress this quality—entertaining.* - John Barr, "American Poetry in the New Century", *Poetry Magazine*, August 23, 2006

What beast is it or jackal-headed god
impressed across the fold says: I and mine
this is, and that, not-I?  What guardian of some line
drawn down the page defines the *fait* and *faut*
of me gone by, embalmed in fine *belles lettres*
or gilt sarcophagi of erudite convention?

May not the Mage whose doleful incantation
bound the Powers to measure and constrain
instead unchain fantastical invention
as steed to bold Creation bear, to bound
at speed across a pained and wearied world,
to heed and heal, inspire and entertain?

I fade to dust silk-wrapped and sealed and set apart—
my essence is vitality; alone where vital is, is art.

## Evening Comes

Evening comes and draws the shades of night
across the windows of my shuddering soul
the day's pains linger in the fading light
each weary breath exacts a teary toll.
So much I have to do is left undone
so much I never wanted done complete
I tremble in an empty room, alone
too tired to try, too blind to see defeat.
Beset by voices I alone can hear
I haunt a face-less wasteland, bleak and bare
prey to passing folly, pressing fear,
mind too numb to dream, or heart to care.
Yet when the darkness strains to quench my sight
your presence sheds a ray of morning light.

# Morning After

*There's more than one way to deal with depression, but each has its consequences.*

When morning comes and yanks the chain of day
And dumps it bright and heavy on my head
I wince and try to make it go away
'Til throbbing temples drive me out of bed.
Remembering stuff I should've done but didn't
Worried about stuff I did but can't recall,
I rise - and then immediately wish I hadn't
Yea, pride and beer both goeth before a fall.
The wonderful world outside I know is calling
If I could just get my carcass off this floor
The flesh is weak - and the spirit is none too willing;
My new life goal is to get through the bathroom door.
But when it seems my day is shot to hell
Your coffee heals my soul, and all is well.

# Rear-view

*Confessions of a workaholic*

When I put a mirror to my past
see my life as others might have seen
the roads not traveled, turnings missed
meandering through a maze of might-have-been
I find I wish I'd had spent less time apart,
played more with my kids, laughed more with friends,
shared more their concerns, bared more my heart,
focused more on means and less on ends.
Though such reflections show the road behind me
long and littered with a life's mistakes
the way ahead, though shorter, may yet find me
clearer for the difference hindsight makes:
While world-won wisdom cannot rearrange
what's been, we treasure still the hope of change.

# Michele'd Better Call Me

*An exercise demonstrating for incredulous students that iambic pentameter is a common rhythm in spoken English.*

Michele'd better call me or she's toast.
She texted me a week ago and said
that she'd be gone a day or two at most –
when she got back she'd tell me what she did.
I haven't heard a thing from her since then –
It's so not like her just to go away –
We're BFFs for chrisake! And since when
Did she not tweet a hundred times a day?
Not knowing is the coldest thing of all.
I'm freaking now, officially – OK?
What if she's lying in some hospital
Somewhere, or worse: run off with Billy Ray?
I bet that's it: she'll come back with a ring
Expecting me to care and everything.

# Masakr u Srebrenici

*In July 1995 more than 8,000 Bosnians, mainly men and boys, were massacred by the Serbian army in and around the town of Srebrenica. When the shooting stopped, wives and mothers were left to find their husbands and children on the killing floors.*

> My youngest boy
> those little hands of his -
> how could they be dead?

# Garden Meditation on Atomic Theory

It isn't my belief
that every bud and leaf
of microscopic billiard balls is made...
that beneath my sharpest vision
they careen with great precision
from collision to collision
in some mystic mechanistic masquerade.

I prefer my childhood stories
where bluebells and morning glories
are the caps of unseen fairies in the grass...
and though I find great consolation
in this wonder-filled creation
yet I fear the situation
(still eschewing gravitation)
where those billiard balls may bite me
in the mass.

# Intentions

*A villanelle*

Whatever thy intentions be
Who darest accost me in my bower
I have no wish to meet with thee.

I turn deaf ears to direst plea
Disturbing thus my prayerful hour
Whatever thy intentions be.

Although with show you promise me
Fine furs and diamonds for my dower,
I have no wish to treat with thee.

I'll not be swayed by bended knee
Nor soulful sigh nor moon-pluck'd flower -
Whatever thy intentions be.

Though thou avow'st eternity
Of passion rapturous in its power,
I have no wish to meet with thee.

Yet - if within thine eyes I see
The light of love all dark devour,
Whatever thy intentions be
I will not wish to part from thee.

## Littered

Litter comes in on little cat feet
to desecrate my carpet and my floor;
my Princess, though fastidiously neat,
her day's ablutions otherwise discrete,
in this respect risks being shown the door.

I take my broom in hand, and, with each rise
and fall of bristled sweep my anger wields,
a steady stream of fierce invective flies
'til Princess turns on me her lambent eyes
and melting *miew*s, and so my hard heart yields.

When I, my ire thus eased, my passions tame,
have laid to rest my impulse to remove her,
I find I can't in conscience place the blame
on her, but on some crass commercial game,
some market ploy by Tidy Cat and Hoover.

Upend your ills, wherever you may find 'em
and underneath some corporate plot's behind 'em.

# In Wildness

*...in Wildness is the preservation of the world. - Henry David Thoreau*

> Please stay on the path -
> this area is home
> to rattlesnakes & poison oak

So says the sign, upright in the brush, consigned
to guide both meandering stroll and headlong rush,
requiring all to stay between the lines
and warning well away from where be monsters.

It's best, they say, for plant and snake – and child
who can't agree?  Plank, paint and stake decree:

> restraint will ward your walk;
> constraint conserve the wild.

Yet pre-forged paths at best lead on
to someone else's goal, to dreams pre-dreamt;
while oaks and streams beyond propound a bound-less
dance, enticing psyches spent with splashing
pools and lofting green exuberance.

And so, off-trail, with those who know
the *tao* of snakes, we're wiled away –
to where contrary spirits find, in wind and stone,
that wildness that unchains the straitened mind,
defies the circumscription of the soul.

## Short-staffed

I miss six inches of my old walking stick
a sturdy shaft of hickory cut green
in an Alabama wood years and years ago
long strong and straight
but for a knot and a skew at the end.

It served me well –
forstalled falls, tended fires,
fended branches, boulders, snakes, bear,
reached often where I could not
supported shelters and weary legs
in and out of nature's grace.

Some time back
in a fit of aesthetic correctness
I trimmed off the knob and the bend at the end -
looked so much tidier there
in the corner by the fireplace.

Now, on the trail again after all this time
I find my fingers go where my staff isn't.

Now, when steps are shorter,
legs stiffer, mountains steeper
I could use those extra inches
whatever they looked like

like I did way back when
when the way things worked
trumped the way things looked.

## Stone

A stone, kicked up along the foot-worn path -
the way into the wild, time out of mind -
amid dry leaves, in sullen sun-specked earth,
a void, a small depression, leaves behind.
The little rock, all angles, lifted from its hole,
awaits some passing boot to be inclined
to shift it.  Here, scrub oak and chaparral
are home; no moss to gather in this brush,
no pressing need for rolling just to roll.
Compare the round arroyo rock, whose hush
is broken by each season's raging run,
and which, by progress, shatters in the crush.
Perhaps it's best, when all is said and done,
to rest, and turn a new face to the sun.

## Legacy

The old church naps,
in cat-upon-the-windowsill repose,
enclosing in its mellowed stones a hush,
a still space in the racing world of rush
and din - and maybe just a quiet dream
of when, in times of gentler need, she shared
the golden hills with sheep, not bared glass,
steel, and speed.

Her solitudes are brief, her slumbers rare,
while from her sandstone spire the chimes
tell out brisk hours, and call those to the busyness
of daily work and prayer, who, levering
heaven's gifts, would open heaven's gate
so hearts of stone may shine, and light
a way for those who, weary, watch, and wait.

Yet sandstone melts in time and blows away
and when someday there's nothing there
but drifts and sage, and pictures on some yellowed page,
can distant lives be monument enough
or distant voices echoing an age?
Can stones still shout when all they are is dust
or bells ring out when rust, sing out
when just a peal of empty air?
The building cannot last. But can the care?

# Vexed

*Owing chiefly to its promiscuous past, the English language blesses us with a dizzying number of ways to say much the same thing.*

I know of no piece of the whole human muddle
more likely to keep our best judgment at bay —
more likely to addle, unsettle, befuddle,
discomfort, disquiet, disturb and dismay;

to bother, bewilder, bewitch, and bamboozle,
to agitate, captivate, exercise, ail,
bedim and bedazzle and frazzle and foozle,
discomfit, distemper, divert and derail;

to cozen and chivy, occlude and confusticate,
mix up and mess up, becloud and bemuse,
to take in, to fake out, disrupt, discombobulate,
diddle, disorient, daze and confuse;

to humbug and buffalo, hoodwink and hornswoggle,
jumble and jangle, beguile and boondoggle,
mortify, mystify, maze, faze and fuss;
confound and discountenance, pother, nonplus,

to freak out, to weird out, to wile and to worry,
to disconcert, discompose, fluster and flurry,
to boggle, to baffle, delude and distress,
to torture, to torment, hagride and harass;

to upset, unhinge us, derange and distract us,
to rattle, alarm us, disarm and impact us,
to feint, fleece and flummox, perturb and perplex,
to devil, unravel and pester and vex —

than sex.

# THREE

## Under Construction

A house half-built I can't pass by
I love the spare frame, bare cement;
that, mid the jetsam of intent,
the tracks of dusty daring lie
where boisterous children laughing came and went.

My house is long since built; yet, in
among old walls of sin and sighs
raised up on hardened dreams, my eyes
at times still catch a gleam from when
a child raced through the dust to claim a prize.

# Agnosia

*Agnosia is a neurological disorder that results in an inability to recognize objects (such as an apple or a key), persons, smells, or sounds despite normally functioning senses.*

There's a place in the brain holding the map
of a perceived object to its sense,
the link of thing to thought.
When broken for example by stroke
or trauma there's often no fuss, no drama –
what *was* simply now is *not*, or is *other*.
The apple in the hand winks, dissembles,
now a starfruit, now a rambutan, exotic
and strange, yet seductively solid and real.

In our minds the map of deed to principle
may too be sundered by trauma or abuse
of power – no flash no thunder,
cupidity *is* fiscal responsibility,
the towering lie *is* truth in the ear
or in the voting booth.

Compassion and common sense
dance desperately but find no place
to hang their meaning.

# Terrible Twos

*Mid-term madness*

A season of non-stop *no*
all stomp and stubbornness
Won't! Can't! Mine! A kicking,
foot-dragging, leg-grabbing whine -
resisting anything good-for-you -
No baff! No begables! No bedtime!
The Terrible Twos are a triumph
of self-assertion over self-interest.
So worrying. Wearing. Intense.
For tots, it's all part of the package;
but must it be so for governments?

# If Only

        if only I'd stayed
    she would not have been alone
       when nothing happened

# Tin Man

*Bewitched by ambition, he bit-by-bit replaces his humanity with a polished persona that terminally isolates him. In that state, he dreams of an intervention that can shake him loose again.*

Me-not-me, stark, still among dark trees
mist-dripped from branch and sullen cloud
by summer's storm and winter's freeze
rust-stalled and -stayed – once proud
I stand for centuries it seems
between the hovel and the fence
unmoving save in fevered dreams
of free limbs, loves, accomplishments.

Successful, but enamored of the chase
my wide-swung axe would slip and where it fell
integrity was stilled, to be replaced
by rationalization's tinny shell
my surface shone, but now inside
no heart, no motive to sustain
engagement with the world, and so I died
to life, to self, to everything but rain.

Where is my Dorothy? Where is my infusion
of innocence and wonder, grit and drive
to wrest me from this desiccate seclusion,
and wake in me the will to be alive?

## Scarecrow

*A long-term worker in a field he doesn't value, wearied by arid sameness and the taunting of peers, he's unsure if it's worse to lose his job or be mired forever in a changeless future. He dreams of liberation and clarity of mind.*

At the cross-roads, neither here nor there
hanging, just a suit of borrowed clothes
straw man in a field of weeds and crows
slow-baked in the dust and stifling air
I wait, because I must, for meager breeze
to ruffle barren thoughts, to speak
some answer to the dark flock's sharp critiques -
no stakes, they come and go with mocking ease.

My once-vigorous brain stuffed to the brow
with hollow answers, wisps of petty lies -
sticks and fluff behind these painted eyes -
no longer do I know what I don't know.
I fear the flame but cannot say
if it's a fiery end I fear the more
or lack of one, and having to endure
the same thing day to day to day.

Where is my Dorothy? When will I hear
the tap of ruby shoes on yellow brick -
they with the power to lift me off this stick
and make my sour and matted mind see clear?

## Pet the Cat

When your life is given lemons
But your lemonade is worse
And your weary work's as welcome
As the moths inside your purse
Just forget about the roses
and the daffodils and that
For peace sublime
Just take the time
To stop and pet a cat

Just stop and pet a cat, my friend
Just stop and pet a cat
For peace sublime
Just take the time
To stop and pet a cat.

When Tai Chi doesn't cut it
And Pilates is a bust
And your therapist is crazy
And your trainer's bit the dust
Render up your top-flight Nikes
And re-furl your yoga mat
For pooling eyes
And plaintive cries -
Just stop and pet a cat.

Just stop and pet a cat, dear one
Just stop and pet a cat
Those limpid eyes
Those plangent cries -
Just stop and pet a cat.

No touch is therapeutic
As the softness of her fur

And no sound's as gently soothing
As the ripple of her purr
Still - her mewing's as annoying
As the whining of a gnat
So if you would
Please be so good
As stop and pet the cat.

Do stop and pet the cat, I pray
Do stop and pet the cat
If you would
Please be so good
As pet the mewling cat.

Her near-incessant yowling
And her howling give me pain
Plus her biting and her scratching's
Slowly driving me insane
Now I know she needs attention
But she needs much more than that
A good swift kick?
A well-placed brick?
Just stop and pet the cat!

Just pet the blessed cat, I beg you!
Pet the stupid cat!
Just lift her by
Her collar, high
Then scratch her tum
And pet her bum -
Just pick her up
And shut her up -
Just pet the friggin cat!

It's all too much - I just can't
take it anymore - hey, where
do you think you're going? -

don't leave me here with
this pernicious feline!
How hard can it be to pet
one sorry excuse for a cat?
And you call yourself
my friend! That's it - no fruit
cake for you this Christmas -
even if this devil-spawn
hasn't driven me into
the looney bin by then -
Listen! I can hear the padded
cell calling me now - "Meeew",
it's saying. "Meeeooooo..."

## You Had Me at Goodbye

They say that absence makes the heart grow fonder
That love will stretch to touch the farthest shore
What distance heals, proximity may hinder
So go away and let me love you more.

# 2 Close 2 Home

*Walking down the road, seeing in the distance a house on fire, a good man does not wish it to be someone else's house. -Jewish proverb*

we think we're good
until the flames
are in our neighborhood

## The Kindness

From somewhere far across an old divide
one day, worn as winters wear,
an enemy of years took me aside
and, leaning close as to confide
some secret, spoke a kindness in my ear.

Some smallish thing it was, some lesser care
but with the sharing of that word
firm walls were shaken, prejudice laid bare
and I - I stifled my reply, for fear
a comfortable enmity be blurred.

We never spoke again.  I never heard
what came of him, nor knew the why
of that small gift; if one reply, deferred,
quashed hope, where, given, might have stirred
the embers of a friendship long gone by.

# Lent

periodically
our lane lines
need restriping

put out the orange cones
and flashing lights - stop
the traffic - blast and clean
rewrite the straight
and narrow

so we, all grab and go,
don't swerve around some
unmarked curve
and crash
and burn

to ashes
the dust from which we come
to which, without direction,
we return

## Medi-cares

Laparoscopical cholecystectomy
Surgeons and nurses converse inrespecttome
Three little holes and they're intheredissectingme
Making what will be a paininthenecktome
'Cause when they're done they'll be handingthechecktome
Laparo-typical chole-cashectomy.

# Poesis

*Work from the pithy middle eye out, swimming in a language sea.* - Jack Kerouac

out of the middle-eye wood
inchoate impulse scrabbles
toward the language sea.

down the beach, words in waves
foam  surge  break – in each
the ocean's every ebb and urge

this is the work:  wade in, sift
the sea-gift swirl, ordain
somehow which go, which stay

so when the last light fades
the polished pearl remains
the drift sands whirl away

# The Tangerine Tree

Orrery for some entropic
universe, dropping amber
planets one by one
the tangerine, succumbing
to some citrusy malaise,
each bare branch raises
with fruitless grace,
the skeleton of leaf-lorn
limbs, like the skull
in an O'Keeffe
talisman against the
sudden empty space.

Yet at its base, among
the fallen orbs, the lone
gardenia, shy and newly shed
of shadows and seclusion,
delights with bright profusion
in the revelation of the sky.

# Small Duties

sometimes
it's one's duty
to show
someone
something
of themselves
that they themselves
cannot see.

some small
beauty,
perhaps, that
the beholder
may have
an eyeful of,
but the beheld
is blind to.

# Don't Speak

*Apologies to Mark Twain*

Open the mouth, not the mind, as a rule,
and you never know what will come out;
better stay silent and be thought a fool
than speak and remove all doubt.

# Given

*Give to those who ask from you, and do not refuse those who would borrow from you. - Matthew 5:42*

I don't need
to hear your
story. You ask,
I give: a given.
God tasks
that of me
whether or no
your so much
need touches
something
soft in me.
Abuse the
gift or use it:
no strings,
it's free. Given
because He
gave before
I asked.

# FOUR

# For A Time

She passed me on the street today,
and, for a time, I thought she'd turn,
and smile, and say my name,
and ask me how I am, and say
how good it is to see me, now,
just when she needs a friend.

And we would walk a little way,
and, for a time, we'd talk
and when we stopped she'd sigh,
and say, why did we, then?
She'd take my hand; we'd walk
away together toward a life
we thought we'd missed.

But she passed by, not seeing –
and, for a time, I thought
I'd call, and reach, and touch,
and she would stop, and turn,
and say my name –

Then she would sigh again,
and turn again, and go,
and, left again, I'd die again,
and so – I left her to her solitude,
and me to mine.

# Barista

*Luscious* comes to mind
as morning-laden eyes
drink in the early-summer
smile, the curve
of sunlit shoulder,
t-shirt scrunched over
levis , unpolished
fingers lading lattes
with unconscious grace.

Nourishing, like loaves
fresh from the oven, or
peaches from a fine old
tree, stirring appetites
as far from lust as Oz
from dust-bowl Kansas,
Persephone in jeans,
long gone the Hadean night,
bestows abundance on
those starving for delight.

# Jonah

Sometimes circumstance
will swallow up decision
and give one time to rethink
one's position. A better-late-
than-never still small yes
can lead one to salvation by
means of whale regurgitation.

# My Kingdom

*Single parenthood, simplified*

My kingdom's very small
two subjects and a castle
not my own - let
against the time I find
I rule myself alone

I am the nest
and till my birds have flown
I'll preen and feed
and see them grow
until they fly -
and flying, soaring
seizing their own sky.

# Governing In The New Millennium

The key to modern
governance is deflection.
To keep the trust, to guard
against disabling disclosure
of major mismanagement
or just pesky indiscretion -
a fiscal misstep, say, or sex -
the superior politician
maintains his or her façade,
elects to have no recollection,
defers fault to the other guy,
to God, or, best, the prior
administration.

## Coasting

You know the feeling.
It's a slow rachet up a steep slope
click   click   click
then you're at the top
and it's a crazy great view
breathtaking
as you whip around those first few curves
then you're jerked around and down
so fast you worry which is worse:
being thrown off the rails and over the side
or losing your lunch and your dignity
all over the sweet person you brought with you.

Then it's just
down   down   down   down
until you hit bottom
where your guts barely have time to regroup
before you start that grinding slog back up again
click   click   click
and you think that if maybe
your car *had* gone off the rails back there
at least you would be headed in a different direction.

Then you turn and see
your kids in the car behind you
having much the same ride
so you go back to inching your way up
that same slope
click   click   click
along with all your other definitionally insane friends
hoping against experience
for a different ride this time.

## 'Twas A Wonderful Life

Now wait a doggone minute, said the newly
late George Bailey as he stood at Heaven's gate.
What - he asked old Clarence, a shining light
in full-fledged native dress - am I doing *here*?
I am - was - forty-two, half a life ahead.  Three kids
to rear, a wife and family to support, a town to help
to grow, as you yourself so clearly showed me
not that long ago - why cut this short?

My boy, the bumptious messenger replied,
it's never been His business to make sense.
Small recompense, perhaps, but here's the truth:
life's length is never measure of its worth.
Just take one look beyond your dear ones' tears
and know the good you'd never trade for years.

## Blow Out

When we try to snuff
an inconvenient thought
there's a gap between
the blow and the out
where the disassociated flame
hangs in the air
away from the wick
looking back perhaps
and thinking: was I there?
Do I return? Or is the call
too strong to anywhere-else-at-all?
Was it enough of a puff
or not?

# Why Talk That Way?

*Inspired by a New Yorker article on poet Li Young Lee*

Why do they talk that way, poets:
all chopped and elusive,
or effusive and obscure?
Why don't they choose
real words, use them like
that gridiron MVP:
We're a team.
We just came to play football.
Hemingway would be proud.

And E. R. Morrow, each day
like Churchill, sending
straightarrow English into
battle for the public heart:
Good night - and good luck.

Why talk that way?
Why each phrase a fight
in flower-infested fields
all things counter, original, strange?
For those who doze face down
in explosive apple blossoms,
it may be all that they can say.

# Fluff

*A refrigerator poem*

Such fluff, she said - a sleepy drunk
in a tiny diamond gown
The musty smell of chocolate
bares my bitter need, reveals
my sad and shadowed life
Lust: drowning in a sea of honey.

# Stopping On The Verge Of An Intimate Evening

*I blame Robert Frost*

I want to be alone tonight,
Slip on my nightdress, douse the light,
and rest in blessed loneliness,
while dreams and fantasies take flight.

I'm often joined, I must confess,
by man-friends helping me undress,
anticipating bliss to come,
the cozy cuddle, sweet caress.

Though all too often I succumb
to wantonness, and bring one home,
They're seldom men I want to keep.
They take my time and leave me numb.

The night is lovely, dark and deep,
And I have solitude to keep,
So males must go before I sleep.
All males must go before I sleep.

## Market Ethics

Why do I feel guilty?
No child is being abandoned, no puppy
kicked. Nothing stolen, envied, killed.
As sins go, it's not high on any god's list.

Who knows? Who sees? Who cares?
There is no proximate accountability
for such a minor lapse. Why should there
be shame? Why worry if you can't get caught?

Is it cultural? I can't picture French friends caring
or Italians at all concerned. Chinese, however, may
find they're disrespecting the people's perfect order
and risking reeducation in the fields.

Is it the do-unto-others heritage, the I'm-third sensibility
of my long-since-relativized Baptist childhood?
What is it in this petty act that I would even call it *sin*?
*Whoso knoweth to do good but doeth it not...*

Maybe in some recess of my social mind I fear
adding to the onus of some worker's daily labors
or skewing someone's lifeline by the time
and energy it takes to right my selfish indiscretion.

The unintended consequences of what,
to me, is one small, if care-less, deed
loom large, for in the deep down dark I know
I bear the balance of the universe.

And so it goes
overwhelmed by the folly of absolving myself
of that which should need no absolution
I turn back, and roll the shopping cart to the rack.

## War & Peace

I've never read War and Peace.

In my youth it was just too long a journey
for a dyslectic to embark on.
Even after I made friends with words
and spent all spare hours in books,
my reluctance lingered. I had seen *Dr. Zhivago*.
I sat through *The Cherry Orchard*. Mostly awake.
With those and nesting dolls and borscht, I figured
I knew everything I needed to know about Russia.

In time I confessed this to my Significant Other.
Imagine my lack of surprise when on my next birthday
she gave me a beautiful leather-bound copy,
gold embossed, supple calfskin, thin paper
like they use in Bibles. Still thick as a cinder block.

Inscribed on the flyleaf in a flowing hand,
"To my darling daughter on your sixteenth birthday:
more about the human condition than I hope
you will ever need to know. Love, Dad." (Not me.
I'm nobody's daughter and way past sixteen.
The S. O. is cultured but cheap.)

I made a real effort to read it.

On planes, in waiting rooms. Always with me.
Vacations, business trips, conferences.
(But not the beach or the bath - the S.O. forbade it.
I left it on the coffee table to impress friends
until it was used as a coaster once too often.)

With all that opportunity, I got up to maybe page
twelve.

I didn't want to not read it, but the concatenation
of negatives confounded even my shrink,
who told me unequivocally that had I spent half the
time reading that I spent worrying about *not* reading
I would have nothing to worry about.

Eventually the S.O. took this failure as a referendum
on our relationship and left with a ski instructor,
a handsome hunk without a reflective bone
in his chiseled body.

So here I am, slumped in my chair, awash in defeat,
my feet up on an impressive gold-embossed
supple calfskin Bible-paper footstool
containing wisdom about the human condition
I'd hoped I'd never need to know.

# Index of Poems

| | |
|---|---|
| 2 Close 2 Home | 47 |
| Afternoon Nap | 19 |
| Agnosia | 38 |
| Barista | 60 |
| Blow Out | 66 |
| Brahman | 14 |
| Canyon Crows | 4 |
| Cartouche | 20 |
| Coasting | 64 |
| Don't Speak | 54 |
| Evening Comes | 21 |
| Fluff | 68 |
| For A Time | 59 |
| Garden Meditation On Atomic Theory | 26 |
| Given | 55 |
| Goodbye And | 9 |
| Governing In The New Millennium | 63 |
| If Only | 40 |
| In Wildness | 29 |
| Intentions | 27 |
| Jonah | 61 |
| Joseph | 6 |
| Legacy | 32 |
| Lent | 49 |
| Littered | 28 |
| Market Ethics | 70 |
| Masakr u Srebrenici | 25 |
| Medi-cares | 50 |
| Michele'd Better Call Me | 24 |

Morning After ................................................................ 22
Morning Tale ................................................................. 12
My Kingdom .................................................................. 62
Nona Nods .................................................................... 10
Paradise Retained ............................................................ 8
Pet the Cat ................................................................... 43
Poesis ......................................................................... 51
Pulling Weeds on an Autumn Afternoon ................. 13
Rear-view ..................................................................... 23
Scarecrow .................................................................... 42
Short-staffed ................................................................ 30
Sierra .......................................................................... 15
Small Duties ................................................................. 53
Stone ........................................................................... 31
Stopping on The Verge Of An Intimate Evening ..... 69
Terrible Twos ................................................................ 39
The Kindness ................................................................ 48
The Tangerine Tree ........................................................ 52
There Is A Place ............................................................. 3
Tin Man ....................................................................... 41
'Twas A Wonderful Life .................................................. 65
Under Construction ....................................................... 37
Vexed .......................................................................... 33
War & Peace ................................................................. 71
Why Talk That Way? ...................................................... 67
You Had Me At Goodbye ............................................... 46

www.ingramcontent.com/pod-product-compliance
Lightning Source LLC
Chambersburg PA
CBHW020949090426
42736CB00010B/1338